DECADES

The SEVENTIES

Michael Garrett

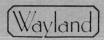

Wayland

DECADES

JS

The Fifties
The Sixties
The Seventies
The Eighties

First published in 1989 by
Wayland (Publishers) Ltd
61 Western Road, Hove
East Sussex BN3 1JD, England

© Copyright 1989 Wayland (Publishers) Ltd

Edited by Roger Coote
Designed by Helen White
Series Consultant: Stuart Laing
Dean of Cultural and Community Studies
University of Sussex

British Library Cataloguing in Publication Data

Garrett, Michael
The Seventies, – (Decades),
1. Western world, Society
I. Title II. Coote, Roger III. Series
909.098210828

ISBN 1 85210 724 3

Typeset by Direct Image Photosetting Ltd
Hove, East Sussex, England
Printed in Italy by G. Canale and C.S.p.A., Turin
Bound in Belgium by Casterman S.A.

Contents

Introduction

In many ways the seventies are still too recent to get a clear picture of what happened and why. Our perspective on the twenties, thirties, and even the fifties and sixties is fairly clear. With the seventies it is still difficult to see the picture as a whole.

People like to give names to all sorts of things, and decades are no exception; we talk about the 'roaring twenties' and the 'swinging sixties', for example. Yet not everyone was a 'flapper' in the twenties or a 'swinger' in the sixties. In fact, many of the important events and trends in history pass a great number of people by. Nonetheless, these nicknames give us a very rough idea of the character of a decade.

Above Motorists experienced petrol shortages as a direct result of the oil crisis. Queues at petrol stations became a familiar sight.

So what is the word to best describe the seventies? There is no doubt that people were more pessimistic than they had been in the previous decade. In the sixties anything had seemed possible. Optimism was high and young people believed they could change the world — through politics, through music, through love and peace. By contrast, the seventies were years of reassessment and doubt. By 1970 many sixties heroes had disappeared. President John F. Kennedy and civil rights campaigner Martin Luther King had been assassinated. Musicians Janis Joplin, Brian Jones, Jimi Hendrix and Jim Morrison were dead through drink and drug abuse. The break-up of the Beatles in 1971 was symbolic of the end of a decade of hope — and the beginning of an era of worry and disillusionment. After the swinging sixties came the uncertain seventies.

The oil crisis beginning in 1973 formed a background to much of the decade, bringing rising inflation and unemployment to the whole of the Western world. Teenagers could no longer be certain of a job when they left school.

There was an overall lack of direction to the decade. Attention turned away from politics and the belief that 'we can change the world'. Instead there was a move towards self analysis: 'What am I? Who am I? Where am I going?' People became more concerned with themselves and less with their fellow human beings.

On a more positive note relationships between the superpowers improved with the signing of the Strategic Arms Limitation Treaty (SALT 1) in May 1972. The Vietnam War finally ended in 1975. People became more conscious of what they were doing to the world they shared with other animals — 'Save the Whale' was one of the big seventies conservation campaigns

The Women's Liberation movement gained strength. Germaine Greer first published the 'bible' of feminism, *The Female Eunuch*, in 1970 and during the decade women started to become more independent. Teenage girls were less likely to follow blindly in their mothers' footsteps or accept their 'place' in society — usually in the home — without question.

Above all, people still had fun in the seventies. Crazes came and went. Among them were 'click clacks' — two balls on a string which you bounced together — chopper bikes, skateboarding, windsurfing and roller discos. Changes in fashion and music, especially punk, kept everyone on their toes. The seventies may have been uncertain but they still had their moments.

Below Roller discos combined the excitement of roller-skating with the energy of disco music. Over-enthusiasm caused many a sprained ankle!

Fashion

The seventies was a decade searching for an image. Various fashion styles were borrowed and adapted from previous eras and there was a fifties revival, inspired by the film *Grease* in 1978, a twenties revival, and even a 'mod' revival reflected in the success of the film *Quadrophenia* in 1979 and 'new mod' pop groups, such as the Jam.

Hot pants were fashionable early on. They were really a continuation of the idea of the miniskirt which had been all the rage in the sixties. Worn with long 'maxi' coats and

Above Hot pants, often worn with high platform heels, exaggerated the 'leggy' look. Many women found the style too revealing.

thigh-length boots, girls also twinned their hot pants with cartridge belts and platform shoes with very high heels. Platforms were designed to make legs look longer and short people taller. They were worn by both sexes, with flared trousers cut to widen from the knee or with Oxford Bags inspired by loose-legged trousers worn in the thirties.

The unisex look which began in the sixties remained popular in the seventies. Men and women dressed more alike than at any other time this century, and children's clothes became more adult-looking, too. In the sixties fashion had become geared to teenagers; now even 8 to 12 year-olds could have their own look.

Denim jeans became almost part of a uniform, and many people from the age of 8 upwards had at least one pair in their wardrobe. Jeans were not only unisex; they also appealed to people of all ages and classes. The denim influence spread to other kinds of clothes. Dungarees and boiler suits became fashionable towards the end of the decade, and hats, caps, shoes and belts were also made in denim.

GI Joe and Annie Hall

Military uniforms were combined with other fashionable accessories. Young people liked the strong image of the clothes if not the harsh realities of war. Khaki or camouflaged US-style caps were worn with long hair. Military shirts with fake badges were teamed with camouflage trousers and gym shoes or fashionable leather boots. Pop group Roxy Music did much to popularize the image with their 'GI look', created for them by designer Anthony Price in 1975.

The Annie Hall look, worn by Diane Keaton in Woody Allen's 1977 film of the same name, inspired many women. The style was

masculine, featuring tweed jackets worn over high-collared shirts and baggy trousers. The fashion-conscious woman of the late seventies wore her clothes baggy, with

Below Diane Keaton and Woody Allen in a scene from the film *Annie Hall*. So-called 'masculine' styles were popular for much of the decade.

Fashion

Below Military-style uniforms and insignia became highly fashionable among young people. Worn with long hair and jeans, the effect was distinctly un-soldierlike.

several layers one over another. Peasant styles and fabrics became increasingly popular, too.

Towards the end of the decade there was a reaction against the military look and other masculine styles. Women looked for clothes that were feminine and flattering. Laura Ashley captured the mood with her blouses and dresses in Victorian prints and small flower designs.

Glam and punk

As in previous decades, music had great influence on fashion in the seventies. Early on, 'glam' rock led to a craze for glittery, colourful costumes, and hair dyed bright green or orange. Large gangster-style hats and theatrical fox furs became highly desirable items. David Bowie's glam style was widely copied by his fans who were known as Bowie boys (and girls).

Punk was perhaps the most original style of the decade. It was a reaction against glam and so-called 'designer' fashions. Punks deliberately dressed to shock. They wore 'urban garbage', including bin liners and empty sweet packets held together with staples. T-shirts and bondage trousers were deliberately slashed. Handcuffs, bicycle chains and razor blades were used as fashion accessories. The safety pin, sometimes worn through the nose or cheek, became a powerful punk symbol. Punks dyed their hair orange, green or purple then either shaved it in mohican style or teased it into a multicoloured 'cockscomb' held in place with soap or lacquer.

Below Laura Ashley's delicate prints appealed to women who wanted to look pretty and feminine. Many of her designs harked back to the Victorian era.

Above Zandra Rhodes was attracted by the originality and creativity of punk fashions. Her designs managed to combine punk style with a sense of humour.

Above A late-seventies punk couple photographed in London, showing many typically punk features — flamboyant hair-styles, tattoos, slashed trousers and shirts, and studded leather.

The vast majority of teenagers were not punks, not least because the style was too outrageous for many. Yet punk fashions did have a lasting effect. Designers such as Vivienne Westwood and Zandra Rhodes were inspired by punk ideas, and both continued designing highly original clothes throughout the seventies and eighties.

Hair

Hair-styles were more varied than in the sixties, though not all were as startling as those of the punks. Women had become more independent and less likely to copy styles that did not suit them. Updated versions of the long bobs of the thirties and forties were reintroduced and Farah Fawcett, star of the TV series *Charlie's Angels*, inspired thousands of lookalikes.

Layered styles, like the 'Rod Stewart' and the 'onion cut', were popular among teenagers. The 'wedge', so-called because of its distinctive 'flying V' shape, became the style for those who were in the know.

Men's hair-styles started off rather long and untidy but got progressively shorter. By 1978 relatively neat, clean-cut styles with long sideburns were common.

Pop Music

The Beatles gave their last live perform-ance in 1970, on the roof of the Abbey Road recording studios in London. The break-up of the group the following year marked the end of an era. The Woodstock generation of the sixties had believed that the world could be changed for the better through music, peace and understanding, but by the beginning of the seventies the dream was in tatters. The Rolling Stones' 1969 free concert in Altamont, California, was meant to be a celebration of rock'n'roll. In fact, it was a disaster. A young black man was stabbed to death by Hell's Angel 'bodyguards' in front of thousands of spectators. The age of innocence was over.

Above Lead singer Roger Daltrey as the deaf, dumb and blind 'Pinball Wizard' in the Who's rock opera *Tommy*.

Pop Music

Above Elton John was known as much for his outrageous stage costumes, and his legendary collection of spectacles, as for his undoubted musical talent.

Art rock and glam rock

At the beginning of the seventies rock music became more self indulgent. Straightforward rock was out and 'art' was in. Following the release of the Beatles' *Sergeant Pepper's Lonely Hearts Club Band* album in 1967, 'serious' rock musicians began to see themselves as artists. The Electric Prunes recorded a version of the Catholic Mass; the Who wrote and performed a 'rock opera', *Tommy*; and rock bands used symphony orchestras and brass bands more and more on their albums. The serious tradition was carried on into the seventies by bands such as Pink Floyd, Genesis and King Crimson.

Glam rock was an extension of art rock but it took itself less seriously. The music was theatrical, and stage performances became a mixture of Hollywood-style glitter and good old-fashioned rock'n'roll. Performers like Mark Bolan and Elton John created images that owed more to Mae West, Busby Berkeley and Liberace than anything that had happened in the sixties.

In time glam rock split into two camps. Bands like Roxy Music appealed to a slightly older audience with their more sophisticated sound. T. Rex, Gary Glitter and the Sweet were more 'pop'. They appealed to younger fans and their singles were very successful in the charts. *Ride a White Swan* by T. Rex was one of the great hits of the early seventies.

Bowie

David Bowie probably had more influence on seventies music than any other performer. He was one of the most original and most copied figures of the decade. He began as a glam rocker but changed his image frequently, always a fashion leader rather than a follower. Bowie reacted against the typical 'macho' rock'n'roll image. The various characters he created for himself, including Ziggy Stardust, Aladdin Sane, Mr Newton and the Blonde Führer, were classless and strangely sexless. It was almost as if he were trying to escape from his own personality. The fantasy world he created appealed to many teenagers who felt confused by the 'real' world around them.

Facing page Variously described as a mime artist, transsexual, genius, urban spaceman and rock 'n' roller, David Bowie always managed to stay ahead of the pack and keep everybody guessing.

Weenyboppers

Children were growing up faster in the seventies than during the previous few decades, and pop fans were younger than ever before. The early seventies saw the emergence of so-called 'weenyboppers' — child pop fans often as young as 8 years old.

Pop stars such as David Cassidy, who became famous through *The Partridge Family* TV series, and Donny Osmond had a fanatical following, mainly of very young girls. All the fans needed was a bedroom, a record player and a friend with whom to share their 'secret' love for their favourite pop star. In Britain the Bay City Rollers, a group of young lads from Scotland, were just as popular, and they created a brief craze for tartan clothes. The hysteria at the concerts of these stars was similar to the 'Beatlemania' of the sixties.

Manufacturers were quick to see their chance to make a profit out of this new audience. They turned out David Cassidy pillowcases, Donny Osmond watches and even a Bay City Rollers Monopoly board! Girls' bedrooms were plastered from floor to ceiling with pictures of the young stars.

AOR and disco

AOR, or 'adult orientated rock', was popular throughout the decade, particularly in the United States. The American music industry seemed to have lost touch with the teenage market in 1967 with the success of the Beatles' *Sergeant Pepper* album and more

Below The Bay City Rollers perform for their adoring young fans. Note the trendy tartan flared trousers. Weenyboppers went weak at the knees but the Rollers' fame was short lived.

 Above The Grateful Dead ... live! They had a cult following in the United States among devoted fans nicknamed 'Deadheads'. The band had a reputation for playing marathon concerts up to ten hours long.

adult 'Californian rock' bands including the Grateful Dead, and Crosby, Stills, Nash and Young. Most American music of the seventies was aimed at college students and the over-25s rather than teenagers. AOR was slick, highly arranged music that appealed to older tastes. Bands like the Doobie Brothers, Steely Dan and Little Feat had a huge following. Fleetwood Mac's *Rumours* became one of the best-selling albums of the decade.

Disco music became popular on a worldwide scale after the huge success of the film *Saturday Night Fever* in 1977. Before this, it had a 'cult' following in New York clubs. Disco sounds later influenced eighties bands including Frankie Goes to Hollywood.

Punk

The Who, one of the giant bands of the sixties, were still singing about 'My Generation' in the seventies. But the song's lyrics, 'hope I die before I get old', had acquired a hollow ring. Most of the bands who had been popular in the sixties, including the Who and the Rolling Stones, *were* of another generation, and punks saw them as 'fat cats' who had grown rich and no longer knew or cared what the average teenager wanted.

Punk music was loud and brash, and was played at a breakneck speed that left no time for subtlety. Punk musicians often had little or no idea how to play their instruments, but that didn't matter. In fact, it was part of the point of punk rock — anybody could do it. You didn't have to be a star to be in a band.

The Sex Pistols brought the punk movement to the attention of the general

Above Johnny Rotten, so-called because of the state of his teeth, led the Sex Pistol's musical assault on the unsuspecting British public.

public in 1976. They were interviewed on television and used the opportunity to be as insulting, abusive and uncouth as they could. They wanted to shock people and they succeeded. The following morning the newspapers were full of outraged headlines. The image of the pop star had changed dramatically since the sixties interviews with the Beatles. The 'Fab Four' may have been cheeky but they came over as basically wholesome young men; your mum might like the Beatles, but she certainly wouldn't like the Sex Pistols.

In fact, punk fashion and music owed a lot to New York 'cult' bands, such as the New York Dolls, Patti Smith, and the Ramones, who had been around since the late sixties and early seventies. Later, the raw energy of punk inspired other bands such as the B.52s, Talking Heads and Devo. Perhaps the biggest success of all was the American band Blondie. Their lead singer, Debbie Harry, used her Marilyn Monroe looks to maximum advantage. Known as the 'peroxide pixie' because of her bleached blonde hair, she appeared in teenage magazines all around the world.

As the punk phenomenon lost steam, many bands disappeared without trace. Others, including the Clash and the Damned, adapted and survived well into the eighties.

New wave

New wave music followed on from punk. British bands, such as the Jam, Elvis Costello and the Attractions, and Ian Dury and the Blockheads, built up a following by playing gigs on the London pub 'circuit'. Small independent record labels, including Stiff and Rough Trade, sprang up to promote them. To begin with their records were distributed from the backs of lorries or sold at concerts. Just like the punks, new wave bands started to believe that they could manage their own careers. The power of the 'majors' — the handful of huge record companies which had dominated the music scene for so long — seemed to be threatened. In the end the threat was short lived as the 'small-fish' independent companies either went bankrupt or became

Above The charismatic Bob Marley and his backing band the Wailers were largely responsible for bringing reggae to the attention of a world-wide audience.

Above Blondie's British television debut on the music programme *The Old Grey Whistle Test* shot them to instant stardom. Their music combined the energy of punk with catchy pop melodies.

big fish. The 'Indie' scene did, however, throw up a lot of talent. Elvis Costello went on to become one of the most successful singer-songwriters of the eighties. *New Boots and Panties*, an album by Ian Dury and the Blockheads, was one of the wittiest and most successful releases of 1977.

Reggae

Reggae was a result of the influence of American rhythm and blues on Jamaican music in the fifties. It featured a distinctive beat which relied heavily on the rhythm section of bass and drums. Reggae was first adopted by ethnic Caribbean teenagers in Britain during the seventies. Later on the international success of Bob Marley and the Wailers brought reggae to the attention of white audiences around the world. White bands were also influenced by reggae, notably the Police who combined the style with more 'mainstream' rock melodies.

The Media

The seventies saw a continuation of the trend of the previous two decades — the growth in the popularity of television at the expense of most other media. Increasingly sophisticated technology also made its mark, especially in the areas of television and the cinema. This helped to speed up the process by which the media was becoming less national and more global in its focus.

Above Satellites in space began to beam television pictures all round the world via receiving stations like this one.

TV

The seventies were dominated by advances in television technology. Improvements in satellite communications meant that pictures could be beamed live to most parts of the world in seconds. In 1972 a record 1,000 million people watched the Munich Olympics. The boom in colour TVs greatly increased the appeal of the medium. Video recorders began to enter the home in the late seventies.

In an attempt to boost viewing figures still further, new television series were aimed directly at teenagers and young children. Fantasy series such as *The Bionic Woman*, *The Amazing Spidorman* and *The Six Million Dollar Man* were all very popular. Television was becoming truly international, with some series being screened in several countries. *The Bionic Woman*, for example, was made in the United States and also shown in Britain, Ireland, New Zealand, South Africa, Hong Kong and elsewhere. One of the effects of trying to reach a global market was that programmes became highly 'packaged', with simple story lines and many visual effects.

Above The Bionic Man (half man, half machine) watches anxiously as his fiancée (the Bionic Woman) has her systems checked out.

Sesame Street, *The Electric Company* and *Mr Rogers' Neighborhood* became essential viewing for American children. Cartoons or 'kid vids' like *Josie and the Pussycats* and *The Harlem Globetrotters* were also very popular. In Britain *Blue Peter*, first broadcast in 1953, managed to move with the times, introducing political and topical issues in a way that children could understand. *Magpie* was designed along similar lines to *Blue Peter* and was almost as popular. *Tiswas*, broadcast on Saturday mornings, was a new kind of television show for children. A mixture of slapstick, news items and wacky comedy, it featured, among others, puppet Spit the dog, and Lenny Henry and Chris Tarrant, two procenters who became much more famous in the eighties.

Some people became worried about the amount of time children spent watching television. The 5 to 15 age group was the fastest growing television audience of all. In 1976, 154 American children aged 4, 5 and 6 were asked 'Which do you prefer, television or daddy?'. Amazingly, 45 per cent of them said they preferred TV.

If children were growing up quicker in the soventies, adult tastes seemed to be becoming more childish. Another American survey in 1980 found that of the top fifteen television programmes enjoyed by adults over 18, over half were included in the top fifteen of the 12 to 18 group, including *Family Feud*, *The Muppet Show*, *The Dukes of Hazzard* and *Three's Company*.

Some people saw TV as a kind of sausage machine churning out low-quality programmes in order to capture ratings. Not all television fitted this description though. Some programmes examined social and political issues in an entertaining way. *M.A.S.H.*, about a team of American medics

Below More and more television programmes were being aimed at young children. The 5 to 15 age group was the fastest growing audience of all.

during the Korean War, was a good example. *All In The Family* in the United States and *Till Death Us Do Part* in Britain were both popular comedies which raised issues that had not been tackled before, including racism, feminism, homosexuality and abortion. And *Kojak*, a popular American detective series, dealt with some of the more sensitive issues in crime — drug taking, prostitution and rape — in a responsible way.

Monty Python's Flying Circus was one of the great comedy successes of the decade. The zany humour of John Cleese, Michael Palin and company appealed to all age groups. The funniest sketches, such as the Parrot Sketch and the Cheese Shop were often learned by heart and recited again and again until everyone was thoroughly bored with them! In the United States the Monty Python brand of humour inspired *The Big Show* and then *Saturday Night Live*, which featured young 'crazy' comedians like John Belushi, Dan Ackroyd and Chevy Chase.

Radio

Commercial local radio stations had existed in the United States since the early days of broadcasting. In the early seventies they

Above Eric Idle, John Cleese, Terry Jones and Michael Palin, four members of the successful *Monty Python* team, strike suitably silly poses.

Above Special effects played a huge part in the success of blockbuster films such as *Star Wars*. The robots C-3PO and R2-D2 even had their own fan clubc.

made their first appearance in Britain. Among the first were London's Capital Radio and LBC stations, which began in 1973. Although they were unable to compete with the BBC (British Broadcasting Corporation) in terms of audience figures, they offered specialist programmes focusing on local issues and catered for musical tastes not reflected in the pop music charts. Some shows covered only reggae, for example, or played tracks from albums rather than singles.

Cinema

As in the fifties and sixties, the growing popularity of television continued the decline of cinema audiences during the seventies.

Some people even predicted that the days of the cinema were numbered. But it wasn't dead yet. Film-makers responded to the challenge of television by making spectacular films with a fantasy element to appeal particularly to children. They used sophisticated special effects to give life to superbly designed monsters and aliens. *Jaws* was a huge success in 1975.

Star Wars (1977) was the big blockbuster of the decade, followed closely by *Superman* (1978).

Hollywood was dominated during this period by a new kind of film-maker. Directors like Steven Spielberg, George Lucas and John Carpenter were mostly the products of university film schools. They brought a refreshing new approach to entertainment and a new awareness of young audiences. The box-office success of films like *Close Encounters of the Third Kind* (1977) and *Star Wars* showed that their approach was very popular.

Nostalgia was a feature of several successful films in the seventies, possibly because the decade itself was something of a disappointment. *Grease* (1978), starring John Travolta and Olivia Newton-John, looked back fondly to the fifties, and for a while it inspired a new craze for fifties fashions. *American Graffiti* (1973) painted an affectionate picture of American youth culture in the early sixties, with high school seniors about to leave for college or military service.

On a more up-to-date note, *Saturday Night Fever* (1977) brought disco dancing into the limelight. Set in Brooklyn, New York, it shows teenagers trying to escape from their humdrum existence by achieving fame on the dance floor. John Travolta's gyrations were copied by would-be disco kings and queens all over the world.

Below John Travolta, dancing to the Bee Gees soundtrack for *Saturday Night Fever*, strikes a pose that was to become familiar all over the world.

Magazines

Music papers and magazines such as *Melody Maker*, *New Musical Express* and *Rolling Stone* continued to influence teenage tastes and fashion as they had done in the sixties. Fads came and went; heroes were built up and often just as quickly shot down. In the sixties, Andy Warhol had predicted that everyone would be famous for 15 minutes; as far as the music press was concerned even this seemed too long.

Magazines aimed at specific ethnic groups and covering specialist musical interests started to appear for the first time. *Black Music*, launched in 1973, was just one example. So-called underground comics like *Fat Freddy's Cat* and *The Furry Freak Brothers* had a cult following. Towards the end of the decade, more sophisticated comics aimed at young girls were introduced. *My Guy* and *Blue Jeans* used photo stories to tackle 'serious' teenage issues, although in reality they were all too often of the 'boy meets girl' variety.

Leisure

During the seventies young people were growing up fast, and were exposed to franker, more open attitudes to sex. Television and the cinema both contributed to sex 'education', if in a rather sensationalist fashion. The contraceptive pill first appeared in 1961 but didn't become freely available to younger people until the seventies. Many seventies youngsters were having sexual

Above Skateboarding was relatively inexpensive in terms of equipment and offered an appealing mixture of thrills and athleticism.

relationships at an earlier age than their sixties predecessors, although there was still a lot of ignorance about venereal diseases and the dangers of 'casual sex'. The number of one-parent families grew dramatically during this period.

Yet sex was not such an issue as in the days of 'free love' during the sixties, when it was used almost as a 'weapon' to shock the older generation. Music and fashion, particularly punk, were the weapons of the seventies.

Below During the seventies, some people expressed concern that prescribing the contraceptive pill to teenage girls would encourage a casual attitude towards sex.

Sport

The entry of children into professional sport was a marked feature of the decade. Girl gymnasts Olga Korbut, aged 14, and Nadia Comaneci, 13, became household names all over the world when they won Olympic gold medals in 1972 and 1976. In 1979 the 15-year-old American tennis player Tracey Austin became the youngest ever competitor at Wimbledon. Bjorn Borg was the 'pop star' of tennis. He won a record four men's singles titles in a row at Wimbledon between 1976 and 1979.

After England's soccer triumph in the 1966 World Cup, Bobby Moore's 'golden boys' became national celebrities. There was a growth in the popularity of the sport but it was short lived. In the seventies, football attendances were on the decline. For the first time this century more people were playing the game each weekend than watching it. On the terraces and around the grounds, violence among football supporters was becoming increasingly common.

Amateur sport became more 'serious' and more competitive. The Little League Baseball Association in the United States was run on much the same lines as the professional game. In the mid-seventies it was the largest youth sports programme in the world.

Jogging became enormously popular and tracksuited joggers were seen everywhere. Even American President Jimmy Carter joined in the fun, although his enthusiasm must have been slightly dented when he collapsed during a jog near Washington in 1979.

Below Olga Korbut, the 14 year-old Russian gymnast, celebrates her gold medal in the women's individual event at the Munich Olympics, 1972.

Below Skimming the waves. Some people went windsurfing for pleasure, others entered highly competitive races. In both cases skill and strength were required.

Skateboarding and windsurfing

Skateboarding was a major seventies craze among children of all ages. First seen in California during the early sixties, new improved boards gave the sport more appeal, and it quickly spread throughout the United States. Britain and Europe followed.

Specialist magazines like *Skateboarder* appeared. The sport developed a language of its own. Advanced riders performed 'wheelies', '360s' and 'kickturns'. Some went 'drainpipe riding' for a real thrill. A careless rider was known as a 'bingo'. Difficult rides were nicknamed the 'coffin' (riding on your back), the 'gorilla grip' and 'shooting the duck'.

Skateboarding produced its own professional riders. The superstars were mostly American and started at a very early age. 'Skitch' Hitchcock, otherwise known as the 'Airborne Devil', began when he was 10. At the top, the sport could be very lucrative: in 1976 US $20,000 in prize money was given to the winners of a competition in Long Beach, California. For lesser mortals however, the sport was just very good fun.

Windsurfing, like skateboarding, originated in sunny California. 'Straight' surfing had been popular throughout the sixties, and the addition of a mast and triangular sail added a new dimension. The sport was very exhilarating and became popular among all age groups. Some expert windsurfers performed daredevil stunts, called 'hot dogs'.

Developments in the sport included windskating on land, and adventurous types even went ice sailing on skates, reaching speeds of up to 95 km/h.

Toys and games

The fifties and sixties had seen the rise of the teenager in terms of spending power, and

Above The huge popularity of jogging during the seventies was just one example of an overall trend towards a healthier lifestyle.

Above Arcade video games with a fantasy theme captured the imagination of many children. Would-be space cadets happily blasted invading aliens out of the skies.

manufacturers and advertisers had come to regard them as 'targets'. In the seventies even 8 to 12 year-olds were seen as fair game. Merchandising, the practice of selling articles connected with popular television series and pop and film stars, became a feature of the decade. There were Donny Osmond T-shirts, pens and watches, Kojak lollies, Wombles and Muppets toys and countless others. Star Wars items, developed from the hugely successful movie, were particularly in demand.

Toys and games were becoming more sophisticated as the seventies electronics revolution gained speed. Perhaps one of the most successful of the 'new' toys was 'Simon'. Shaped like a flying saucer, it was a memory game with four coloured lights which had to be pressed in the right order. Electronic tank and battle games were followed, towards the end of the decade, by 'computer' bat and paddle games. More sophisticated arcade games like Space Invaders also appeared.

In spite of this technological sophistication, however, more traditional playthings continued to sell well, and dolls were still among the most popular girls' toys during the seventies.

Youth Cultures

Ever since the days of the Teddy boys and Hell's Angels of the fifties, young people have wanted to stand out from the crowd. Being an individual is not easy, though, especially if, like many teenagers, you are shy and lacking in confidence. The youth cultures that sprang up in the sixties and seventies gave young people the chance to express themselves in terms of the way they looked, the music they listened to, and what they were 'for' and 'against'. More importantly, belonging to a group of like-minded people was a kind of safety net: why stand out alone when you can stand out together?

Above The seventies was a melting pot of ideas, old and new. As a result many different tastes and fashion styles gained acceptance.

Skinheads

In the late sixties, some so-called 'hard' mods developed a new image. They wore heavy Dr Marten boots — known as 'bovver boots' — rolled-up jeans, check shirts and braces. They shaved off their hair and called themselves 'skinheads'. During the seventies, they came to be associated with football violence, racist attacks, particularly on Pakistanis, and violence against homosexuals. Skinheads reacted against the hippy values of the sixties. They were usually working-class boys who exaggerated traditional working-class prejudices. They were often fiercely patriotic, and supported racist organizations such as the National Front and the British Movement.

To be fair to skinheads, not all of them were racist. In fact, Jamaican influenced ska and bluebeat were their favourite types of music.

Rude boys

In the sixties, Martin Luther King and others had argued passionately for racial harmony, and equality among whites and blacks. In the seventies there was very little evidence that this dream was coming true. Non-white teenagers were still being discriminated against. A background of racism, poor job opportunities, police harassment and unemployment led some young blacks to look for an identity of their own beyond the constraints of 'normal' society.

Rude boys or 'rudies' developed from the tradition of the Jamaican 'hustler', like the character played by Jimmy Cliff in the film *The Harder They Come* (1972). A hustler was someone who could not find work, or didn't want to, and earned a living through petty crime. Hustlers were cool and streetwise. British rudies associated with this image.

Facing page Skinheads deliberately cultivated a brutal, violent image – a marked contrast to the hippies who preached peace and love during the sixties.

Below The Specials, a Coventry-based band influenced by 'rude boy' music and style, had several British hits. Later, the nucleus of the band formed the Fun Boy Three.

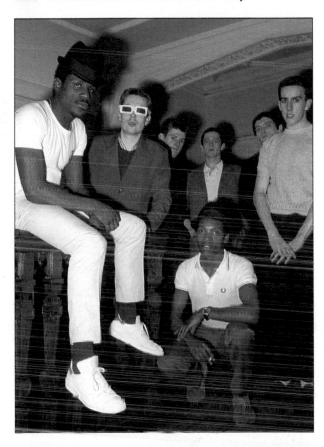

They were often unemployed and frustrated, and the 'glamorous' rudie image gave them a certain style and identity. They copied the 'stingy brim' hats and dark 'shades' (sunglasses) worn by hustlers. They smoked marijuana and passed the time listening to ska and reggae music, playing dominoes and gambling. Some white teenagers adopted the rudie style. In Coventry, the Two Tone record label featured bands like the Specials who had black and white members and took their image from the rudies.

Rastas

Rastas were followers of the Rastafarian religion. They believed that Emperor Haile Selassie of Ethiopia, whom they called Ras Tafari, was a living god, and that one day they would be led out of 'Babylon' (Britain) to Ethiopia, their spiritual home. This belief was particularly appealing to young blacks who saw Rastafarianism as a way of escaping the harsh realities of life in Britain.

Rastas believed that the illegal drug marijuana, which they called ganga, was sacred. This often got them into trouble with the police. The 'Rastaman', with his long 'dreadlocks', woollen cap and Ethiopian colours of red, green and gold, became an important symbol for seventies black youth.

Above Rastafarianism gave some of Britain's ethnic Caribbeans a sense of unity and pride in a shared religion with its own social and moral code.

Punks

Although it was the Sex Pistols who brought punk to the attention of the general public in 1976, the punk movement actually started in the early seventies.

Like other groups, punks were trying to find an identity of their own. Punk developed out of British working-class teenage feelings of not belonging. Unemployment (the highest since the Second World War), boredom, life in huge housing estates and the lack of any real prospects created a sub-culture with its own style of music and dress. Meeting places, clothes shops and makeshift clubs sprang up. Magazines with names like *Sniffin Glue*, *Live Wire* and *Vortex* were produced by fans. Like punk music and clothes, they were deliberately rough and ready. There was nothing slick about the punk phenomenon.

Punks succeeded in offending white middle-class values, which was one of the objects of the exercise. They used fashion, music and style as weapons. Perhaps the most important thing about the punks was that they showed it was still possible to be original. Those who had learned the lesson but become bored with the style went on to create others. The New Romantics of the early eighties, for example, were nearly all ex-punks.

Below To many people punks looked as if they came from another planet, but there was an originality about them which was impossible to ignore.

Seventies Style

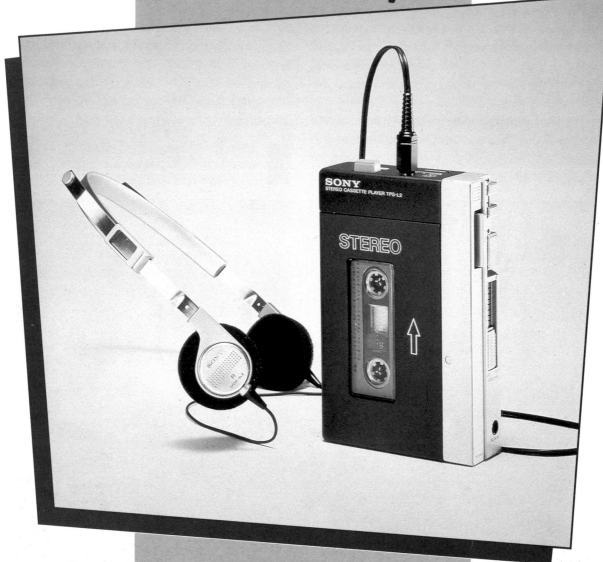

Above Sony launched their Walkman cassette player in 1978. As cheaper models became available personal stereos became enormously popular world-wide.

The fifties and sixties had witnessed a building boom resulting from new construction techniques and the need to create cheap, functional housing and office space. Huge box-like buildings with vast areas of concrete and plate glass were thrown up with little thought as to how practical they were to live or work in. Many were difficult to heat in winter and to ventilate in summer. Huge housing blocks with dimly lit walkways and lifts frequently out of action became centres for vandalism and crime.

Post-modernism

The seventies experienced the legacy of poor planning and bad design. Many buildings had to be demolished as they were literally falling down or had become uninhabitable. On 15 July 1972, the Pruitt Igoe high-rise block of flats in Missouri, USA, was officially dynamited. Built only twenty years earlier, its design proved so hostile and inhuman that people refused to live there. Charles Jencks, a British architect, called this event 'the death of modern architecture', and gave a name to the new movement which was to sweep through all areas of art and design — 'post-modernism'.

The post-modernist movement appeared in the seventies and affected furniture, textiles and other consumer products. Behind it lay a rejection of so-called 'good form' — the idea that art and design had to have some kind of classical style. Just as punk style was anti-fashion, post-modernism was anti-design. Post-modernists believed that everything was up for grabs and they borrowed ideas from different periods of history. They used unusual materials to create dramatic effects and placed familiar objects in strange surroundings. They broke the 'rules' about what was good taste and what was bad.

Below Architect Richard Rogers' design for the Pompidou Centre in Paris was highly controversial. People either loved it or hated it. To some it looked more like a chemicals plant than an arts centre.

Seventies Style

Above Cambridge-based scientist and inventor Clive Sinclair was one of the first people to realize the potential of miniaturization. His pocket calculator was the first in a long line of innovative products.

One of the most celebrated examples of post-modernist architecture is the Pompidou Centre in Paris built by Richard Rogers in 1978. One of the most original is the Best Product Showrooms in Houston, USA, built in 1975 by the SITE Architects group.

Design in miniature

The microelectronics revolution had far-reaching consequences for familiar and not-so-familiar household objects. Electrical components were made smaller and smaller, and this meant that many electronic gadgets could also be smaller. Clive Sinclair invented the first pocket calculator in 1972 and the first mini TV followed in 1975. In 1978 Sony launched their 'Walkman' cassette player. The invention of the silicon chip enabled computer manufacturers to greatly reduce the size of their machines, and the first portable computer became available in 1977.

Habitat and high tech

In the mid-seventies Terence Conran's Habitat chain of shops started to have a real influence on the type of design found in middle-class British homes. By 1975 there were 12 shops around the country, one in Paris and one in New York. Habitat sold good-quality, well-designed furniture and kitchen equipment, influenced by French and Scandinavian designers. In many ways Conran was responsible for making design accessible to more people.

High tech emerged in the seventies and carried on well into the next decade. It was a design style for the home, heavily influenced by the clean lines and simplicity of industrial design. The practice of converting large 'lofts' or warehouses into family homes started in Manhattan, New York. These very spacious apartments were particularly

Above New York subway trains were painted both inside and out by aspiring young street 'artists'. To most people, however, the 'art' of the graffitists was nothing but vandalism.

suited to the high-tech look. Industrial furniture, steel shelving, factory-style lights and hard-wearing rubber flooring gave them a pleasing simplicity and made maximum use of space. High tech was supposed to look empty, and in many ways it was a reaction against the over-elaborate style of forties and fifties homes.

Spray-can art

In the seventies graffiti became increasingly common. It also came to be regarded by some as an artform. Whereas it had once been confined to neighbourhood walls and bus shelters, young 'writers' in New York discovered that subway trains made excellent movable 'canvases' for their designs. They adopted nicknames or 'tags' which were recognizable to their friends if not to the police. 'Taki 183', 'Crash', 'Daze' and 'SAGO' became familiar 'signatures' to New York commuters.

Some of the more talented 'writers', like Vaughn Bode, went on to hold major public exhibitions of their work. However, not all graffiti was art. Most was little more than crude vandalism. The New York subway system and other bodies spent vast sums of money on cleaning graffiti from their property.

Images of the Seventies

Bloody Sunday

Against a continuing background of violence and unrest in Northern Ireland, Brian Faulkner, the prime minister of the province, introduced internment without trial in 1972. This meant that anyone suspected of having committed a violent crime could be held indefinitely. Hundreds of suspects were rounded up and questioned by the security forces. On Sunday 30 January a large anti-internment demonstration in Londonderry was broken up when British troops fired on protest marchers, killing thirteen of them. This day became known as 'Bloody Sunday'. Shortly afterwards the Northern Irish Parliament at Stormont was suspended and the province was administered by direct rule from London.

Above British troops round up protesters in Londonderry, Northern Ireland. The introduction of internment without trial caused a great deal of anger and resentment.

The Munich Olympics

The seventies saw a dramatic increase in acts of terrorism. Groups like the Red Army Faction and Black September sought to achieve political goals through acts of violence often directed at innocent civilians. The most shocking incident happened at the Olympic Games in Munich in September 1972, and was carried out by eight terrorists from the Black September organization. They shot dead two Israeli athletes and took nine hostages. They were demanding the release of 200 Arab hostages held by Israel.

The West German authorities negotiated with the terrorists and moved them and their hostages to a nearby airport, apparently agreeing to fly them to a friendly Arab country. But German marksmen were lying in wait. In the shoot-out that followed, all the hostages and five terrorists were killed.

Below The bodies of the murdered Israeli hostages are flown home from the Munich Olympics in 1972. People all over the world were shocked by the terrorists' fanatical disregard for innocent human lives.

Concorde

Concorde, the world's first supersonic airliner, was a joint Anglo-French project which took over 20 years to get from the drawing board into the air. Its elegant shape and 'droop snoot' nose made it one of the most distinctive, and many would say the most beautiful, aeroplanes ever built. Concorde finally came into service on 21 January 1976. But it was costly to build and to run, and some countries objected to the noise it made as it broke the sound barrier. Very few Concordes were sold, and no more were built after 1979.

Below A British Airways Concorde streaks through a clear blue sky. However, opposition from environmental groups led some countries to ban the plane from flying over them.

Muhammad Ali

Cassius Clay, who later changed his name to Muhammad Ali after becoming a Muslim, was arguably the greatest heavyweight boxer of all time. He first won the world heavyweight title in 1964 when he was 22, taking it from Sonny Liston. Ali's arrogance — his catch phrase was 'I'm the greatest' — his sense of humour and above all his superb, seemingly effortless boxing ability made him internationally famous.

His religious convictions led him to refuse to serve in the US Army during the Vietnam War. As a result he was deprived of his title for three years between 1967 and 1970. During the seventies he regained the title twice, the only heavyweight ever to do so.

The first test-tube baby

On 25 July 1978, Louise Joy Brown was born in Oldham General Hospital, in England. She was the first baby to be conceived outside its mother's womb.

Her mother, Lesley, had once been told that she could never have a child. The successful birth was the result of a collaboration between Oldham gynaecologist Patrick Steptoe and two Cambridge doctors, Robert Edwards and Barry Bavister. They developed a technique by which an egg taken from a woman's ovary could be fertilized in a test-tube by sperm from a man, and then placed back inside the womb to grow. Little Louise, a normal, healthy baby, gave new hope to childless women all over the world.

Above Muhammad Ali fights 'Smokin' Joe Frazier in one of their epic world title bouts. Frazier won the first but Ali gained his revenge in the following two.

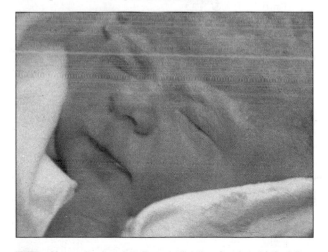

Above Louise Joy Brown shortly after her birth, blissfully unaware of her importance as the world's first test-tube baby.

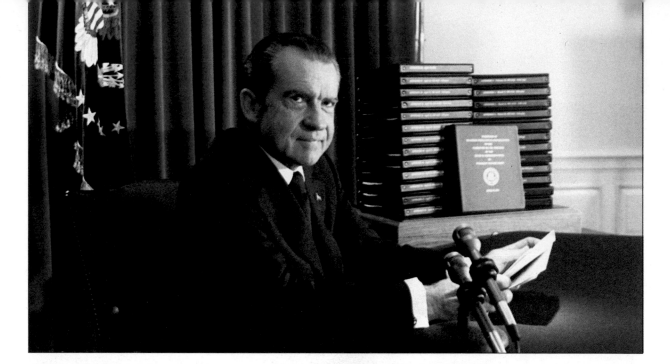

Watergate

The Watergate scandal of the early seventies shocked people in the United States and around the world. At first it seemed little more than an example of petty corruption. In June 1972 five men were arrested after breaking into the Democratic Party headquarters in the Watergate building in Washington DC. They were caught trying to plant electronic surveillance equipment and photographing sensitive documents. Richard Nixon, America's Republican president, denied that he or any of his staff were involved in what he called this 'reprehensible activity'. However, an investigation by the *Washington Post* newspaper indicated otherwise and the Watergate burglars were proved to be connected to the Nixon administration. Nixon himself refused to appear before a Senate Select Committee or to release sensitive tape recordings which may have implicated him in the scandal. His popularity plummetted; Americans were shocked that their president was apparently being dishonest. In August 1974 Nixon finally admitted withholding important information and offered his resignation.

 Above President Nixon taped most of his conversations at the White House, and it was the tapes that were to prove his implication in the Watergate scandal.

Nicaragua

Anastasio Somoza first came to power in the South American country of Nicaragua in 1967. The Somoza regime swiftly acquired a reputation for corruption, extortion and violence against all those who opposed it. Somoza himself reputedly accumulated a fortune of some US \$500 million while in office. In 1973, public discontent grew when it became clear that Somoza had 'diverted' aid sent to help victims of a devastating earthquake to swell his already bulging coffers. Support for the Sandinista National Liberation Army (SNLF) — named after Augusto Sandino, a national hero who had been murdered by Somoza — grew rapidly. A bloody civil war broke out in which 40,000 Nicaraguans died and 75,000 lost their homes. The war ended in 1979 when Somoza fled to neighbouring Paraguay, where he died a short time later.

 Facing page Anastasio Somoza acquired a reputation as one of the most ruthless dictators in South America. He relied heavily on the loyalty of the Nicaraguan Army.

Images of the Seventies

The fall of Saigon

The Vietnam War, one of the longest in modern history, first started in the late fifties. United States involvement began in 1962 when President John F. Kennedy sent 4,000 American 'advisers', and by 1972 350,000 American troops were involved on the side of South Vietnam.

The war became increasingly costly and unpopular. What had initially been seen as a crusade against the evils of Communism (in the form of the North Vietnamese) became a war in which the United States appeared to be in a 'no-win' situation.

The United States finally decided to cut its losses and the last American troops left Vietnam in 1973. In July 1975, Communist troops entered Saigon, the South Vietnamese capital. The few remaining American personnel had earlier been hurriedly airlifted out by helicopter amid scenes of panic and fear. The war was over but the United States had paid a high price — 50,000 American soldiers had been killed.

Below America's decision to pull out of the Vietnam War caused widespread panic as thousands of South Vietnamese refugees tried to escape from advancing Communist troops.

Below The bodies of members of the People's Temple are strewn around the Jonestown commune having obeyed their spiritual leader's order to commit suicide.

Mass suicide at Jonestown

In the mid-seventies the 'Reverend' James Jones founded a religious commune in Guyana. He moved his followers from San Francisco to the South American jungle where he established the People's Temple. Cut off from the outside world, he was able to present himself to the members of his cult as a kind of god. Those who refused to accept his 'divinity' were murdered. Reports of corruption and violence led to an investigation of the cult by a group of United States' politicians and journalists. They were attacked by Jones's followers and four were shot. Realizing that his days were numbered, Jones ordered his followers to commit suicide by poisoning themselves. Those who refused were shot. In all, 913 members of the Temple died in November 1978, including Jones himself.

Three Mile Island

In the seventies nuclear power was seen by many people as a solution to the growing energy crisis. Others were concerned about the dangers of potentially catastrophic accidents in nuclear power stations. One such accident occurred in the United States at the Three Mile Island nuclear plant near Harrisburg, Pennsylvania, on 28 March 1979. A small amount of radioactive gas was released into the atmosphere. The population of Harrisburg and the surrounding area was evacuated. Fortunately no one was seriously hurt but it became obvious that nuclear power plants were not as safe as they were claimed to be. A Nuclear Regulatory Commission study later revealed that the reactor at Three Mile Island was within 60 minutes of a 'meltdown' which could have caused thousands of deaths.

Above A major disaster was only narrowly avoided at Three Mile Island in the United States. Anti-nuclear protesters saw the incident as a warning of the dangers of nuclear power.

Images of the Seventies

Idi Amin

Idi Amin was an ex-army sergeant who rose to become the self-appointed Life President of Uganda during the years 1971 to 1979. His enormous physique and 'unconventional' style — he had 6 wives and 20 children — made him a figure of fun to much of the Western world.

Inside Uganda, however, Amin ruled with appalling savagery. During his time in office more than 350,000 Ugandans were murdered as 'political opponents'. It was one of the bloodiest chapters in Ugandan history.

Revolution in Iran

1971 marked the 2,500th anniversary of the Persian monarchy. At that time the Shah of Iran could have been forgiven for believing that his position on the throne was secure. His handling of Iran's economy had created enormous wealth and the general standard of living had improved considerably since he came to power in 1953. However, other forces were at work.

Iran is an Islamic country and its people are deeply religious. The mullahs — Islamic religious leaders — objected to the Shah's 'modern' approach. They preached Islamic fundamentalism and a return to the teachings of the Qur'an. In 1979 the 79-year-old Ayatollah Khomeini returned to Iran from exile in Paris and was given an ecstatic reception. He demanded the removal of the Shah and a return to pure Islamic values. In January the Shah was forced to bow to public pressure and he left the country.

Left Many Westerners regarded Idi Amin as a rather comical figure. But beneath his pompous self-importance lay a brutal dictator. In 1979 Amin fled when his country was invaded by Tanzanian troops and Ugandan exiles.

Facing page On his return to Iran from exile, the Ayatollah Khomeini was greeted by huge crowds of supporters.

Glossary

AOR (adult orientated rock) A term used to describe rock music (usually American) which is more sophisticated than the normal pop single.

Bluebeat (and ska) Music that came originally from Jamaica and was brought to Britain by Caribbean immigrants in the fifties.

Bondage trousers Punk-style trousers with many zips, straps and chains for decorative effect.

Busby Berkeley A 1930s director of Hollywood musicals who was known for his lavish dance routines and set designs. Berkeley's style inspired glam-rockers such as Elton John and Bryan Ferry.

Civil Rights Rights which belong to everyone in a free society, such as the right to vote and the right to a fair trial. The civil rights movement in the United States aimed to win these rights for black citizens.

Communism A political theory aiming to establish a society where the major enterprises such as factories, mines, farms and shops are owned by all citizens rather than a class of wealthy people. In practice, Communist societies have tended to create powerful state authorities which control those enterprises.

Contraceptive A device used to prevent an unwanted pregnancy. The contraceptive pill for women became available in the sixties.

Cult In fashion terms, a small group of people who appreciate the same style and group together to be different from more 'mainstream' fashions. In religious terms, members of a sect, often following one powerful individual.

Divinity The state of being god-like.

Droop-snoot The name given to the long, pointed nose of Concorde, which can be lowered during take-off and landing to give the pilot better visibility.

Feminism The movement aiming to win full rights and respect for women in society, and to celebrate the special qualities of the female sex.

Flapper A name for a fashionable young woman of the twenties.

Functional Something designed to work efficiently rather than to look attractive.

High tech A design style which uses industrial-style objects and furnishings in the home.

Gig A pop or jazz music concert.

Graffiti Drawings, names and messages scribbled or painted on walls, advertising posters, etc. In the seventies New York's subway trains became targets for graffiti 'writers'.

Hell's Angels Groups identified with high-powered customized motorbikes, and sometimes associated with gang violence.

Indie Short for independent; a word used to describe the small record labels that sprang up in the seventies to promote new wave bands.

Inflation The rate at which the price of goods and services increases. When inflation is high, prices rise very quickly.

Internment Detaining or imprisoning people, especially during wartime.

Macho A word to describe fashions and behaviour which make men look tough and aggressive; from the Spanish world *machismo*.

Marijuana An illegal drug derived from the hemp plant.

Mods Fashion-conscious working teenagers who emerged in Britain during the early sixties.

Nostalgia Looking back to the past with affection, in the belief that life was better then than it is today.

Oil crisis The world-wide economic crisis brought on when Arab oil-producing nations doubled the price of oil and cut its production. Many countries became short of oil, industrial production fell, and inflation and unemployment rose sharply.

Optimism A tendency to expect the best.

Patriotism Pride in one's own country. Although skinheads frequently claimed to be patriotic, this often became an excuse for racial hatred and violence.

Pessimistic People who always expect the worst are said to be pessimistic.

Unemployment The condition of being out of work.

Unisex Clothes designed to be worn by either sex.

Venereal disease (VD) Disease passed from one person to another during sexual intercourse.

Woodstock A town in New York State, USA, where a huge open air rock music festival was held in 1968.

Further Reading

The Seventies, John Edwards (Macdonald Educational, 1980)

The Seventies, Tim Healey (Franklin Watts, 1989)

The Design Source Book, Penny Sparke and others (Macdonald, 1986)

Growing Up in the 70s, Nance Lui Fyson (Batsford, 1988)

The Cartoon History of Rock and Roll, Serge Dufoy and others (Elmtree, 1986)

Modern Times, Peter York (Futura, 1984)

The Movies of the Seventies, Anne Lloyd (Orbis, 1984)

The History of Television, Rick Marschall (Bison, 1986)

The Guinness Guide to Twentieth Century Fashion, David Bond (Guinness, 1981)

General background

The Penguin Book of Twentieth Century History, 1900-1978, Alan Palmer (Penguin, 1978)

Chronicle of the Twentieth Century (Longman, 1988)

Picture Acknowledgements

Barnaby's Picture Library 10, 18, 25t, 25b, 27; Camera Press 30 (Lennox Smillie), 35 (Willy Spiller), 40 (Ollie Atkins), 44 (Richard Lindley), 45 (J. Haillot/L'Express); Daily Telegraph Colour Library 34 (Patrick Ward); Kobal Collection 7, 19, 21 (Lucasfilm Ltd); Photri 8t, 20t, 23, 43t; Popperfoto 24b, 36, 37; Redferns 12, 14, 16b; Rex Features 4, 5, 6, 11, 13, 15, 16t, 22, 24t, 26, 28, 29, 31, 39t, 39b, 42; Sony UK 32; TOPHAM front cover, 8b, 9, 17, 20b, 33, 38, 41, 43b.

Index